GET READY
FOR CHORD AND ARPEGGIO DUETS!
BOOK 1

by Wynn-Anne Rossi and
Lucy Wilde Warren

CHORD AND ARPEGGIO DUETS

INSTRUCTIONAL ACTIVITY PAGES

Pickled Peppers in C

Secondo

Adapted by W. Rossi

Pickled Peppers in C

Primo

In the primo parts throughout this book, measures 3–10 and 19–22 may be practiced hands separately until comfortable.

Crashing Waves in G

Secondo

W. Rossi

Crashing Waves in G

Primo

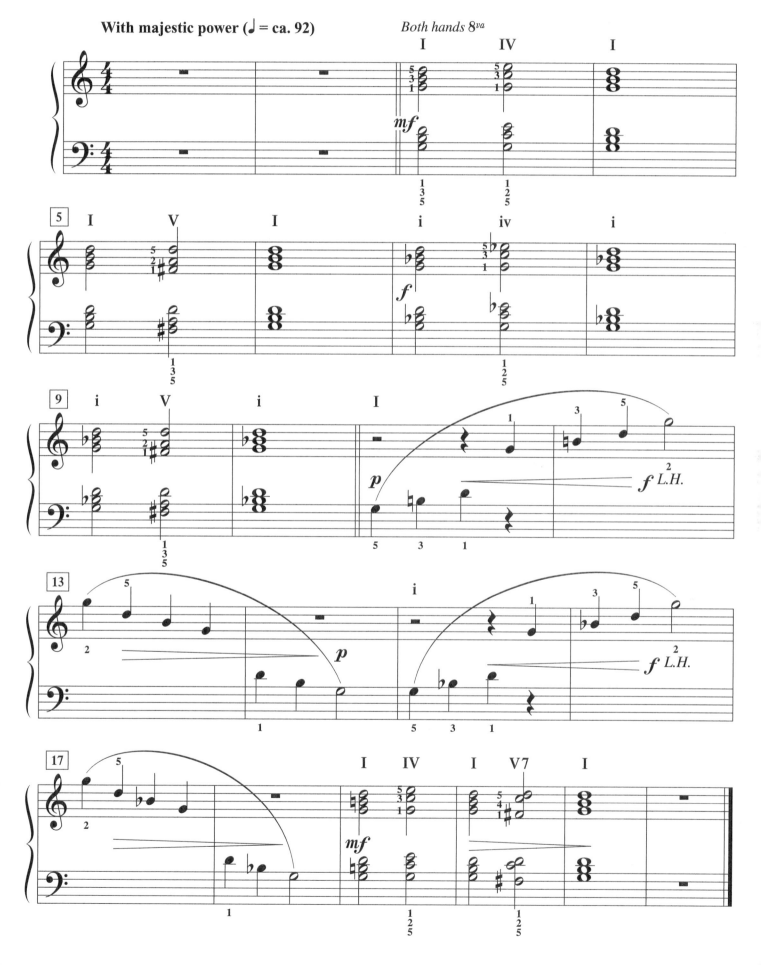

Stormy Breezes in D

Secondo

W. Rossi

I1316

Stormy Breezes in D

Primo

Train's Comin' in A

Secondo

W. Rossi

Train's Comin' in A

Primo

Rhino Blues in E

Secondo

W. Rossi

Plodding along (♩ = ca. 120)

Rhino Blues in E

Primo

Rock the Party in B

Secondo

W. Rossi

Rock the Party in B

Primo

Scary Shark in F♯

Secondo

W. Rossi

Scary Shark in F♯

Primo

Bingo Barks in F

Secondo

Adapted by W. Rossi

Bingo Barks in F

Primo

Heavy Boots in B♭

Secondo

W. Rossi

Heavy Boots in B♭

Primo

Her Majesty in E♭

Secondo

W. Rossi

Her Majesty in E♭

Primo

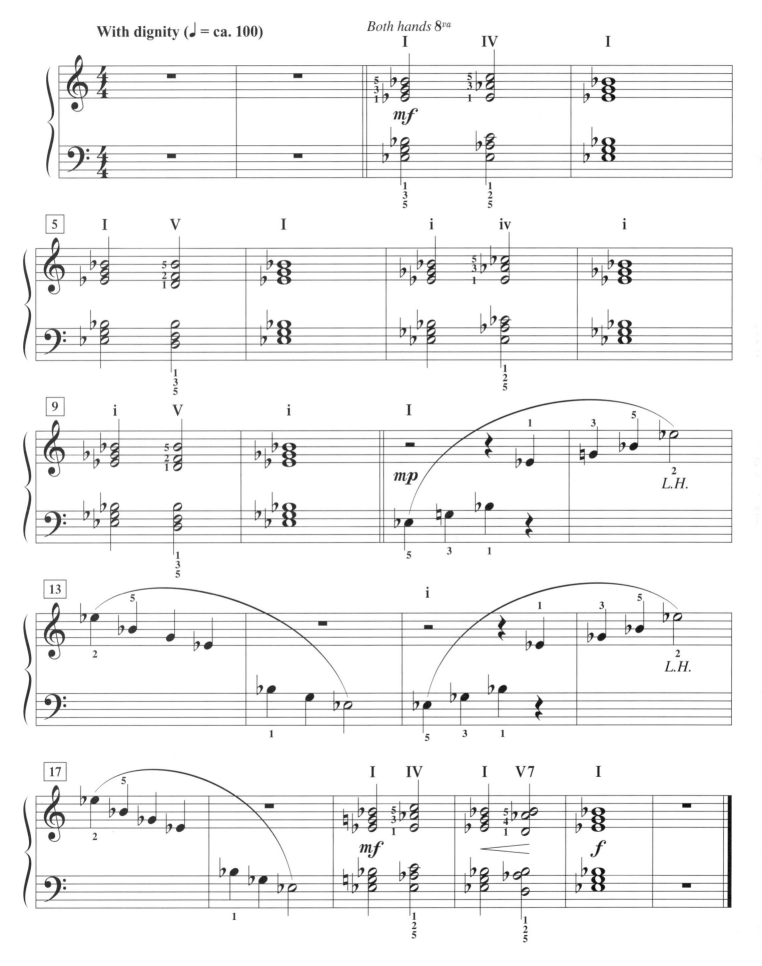

Spider Webs in A♭

Secondo

Adapted by W. Rossi

Spider Webs in A♭

Primo

Cat & Mouse in D♭

Secondo

W. Rossi

Cat & Mouse in D♭

Primo

Constructing Chords and Arpeggios

Major and minor chords are the most common forms of harmony used in Western music.

One way to build major and minor chords is to use the *root, 3rd,* and *5th* notes of major and minor scales.

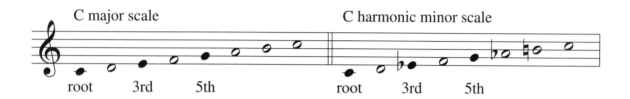

Another way to build chords is to count half steps:

In a *major chord,* there are **4 half steps** from the root to the 3rd, and **3 half steps** from the 3rd to the 5th:

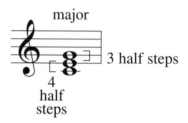

In a *minor chord*, there are **3 half steps** from the root to the 3rd, and **4 half steps** from the 3rd to the 5th:

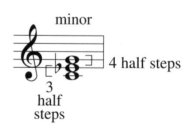

An **arpeggio** is a chord that is played one note at a time. It is played from bottom to top, or top to bottom.

In this book, you will be playing *major arpeggios* (built on major chords) and *minor arpeggios* (built on minor chords).

Acrobatic Arpeggios

Imagine that you are "tumbling in space" as one hand crosses over the other to play the arpeggios below. Listen to decide whether each arpeggio is **major** or **minor.**

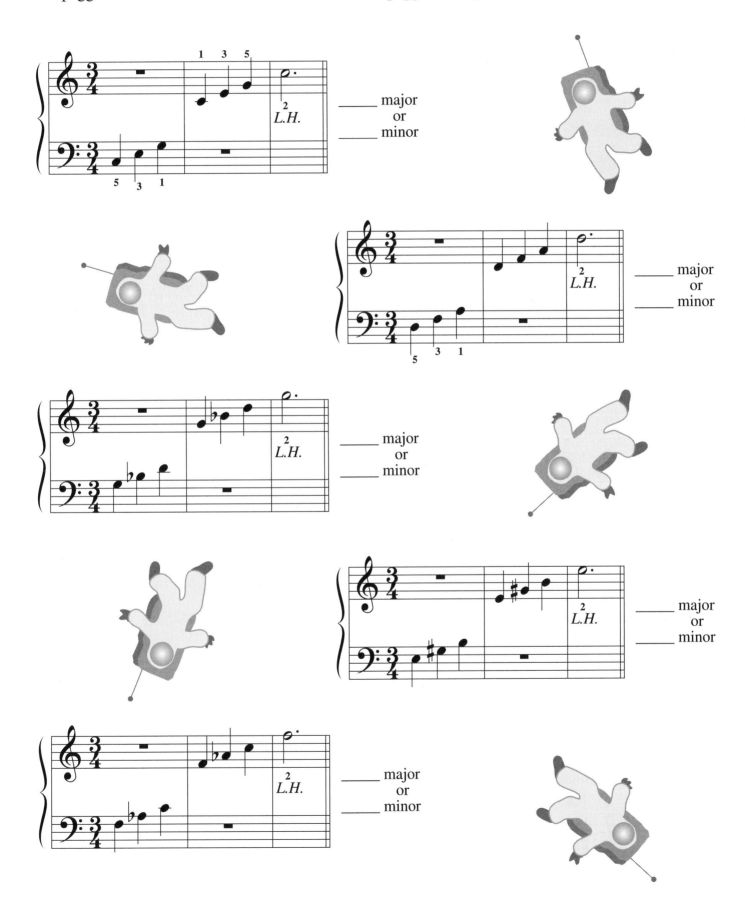

_____ major
or
_____ minor

_____ major
or
_____ minor

_____ major
or
_____ minor

_____ major
or
_____ minor

_____ major
or
_____ minor

Calling All Cadences...

Cadences are groups of two or more chords. These groups of chords are used as punctuation, much like commas or periods, at the ends of phrases or sections in music.

Two of the most common cadences are **I-IV-I** (1-4-1) and **I-V-I** (1-5-1). The chords used in these cadences are built on the 1st, 4th, and 5th notes of a major scale:

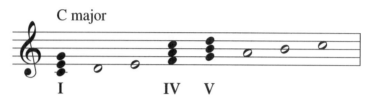

At least one of the chords in each cadence may be *inverted* (its notes rearranged) to make the cadence easier to play and to create a smoother sound.

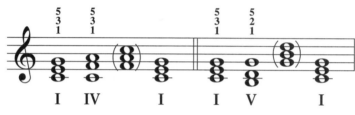

A variation of the I-V-I cadence is the **I-V7-I**, in which a 7th is added above the V chord:

When the V7 chord is inverted, the 5th is usually left out to make the chord easier to play.

It's a Minor Thing

In minor keys, the **i** and **iv** chords will be minor, but the V chord will still be major. Minor cadences are built on the notes of the harmonic minor scale.

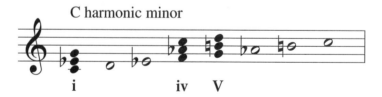

Here are minor versions of the three cadences that you have learned:

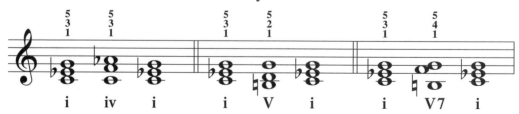

I'm All Ears!

Listen as your teacher plays each of the cadences below, in any order. Point to each one as you hear it. For a challenge, try identifying these in a variety of keys with your eyes closed!

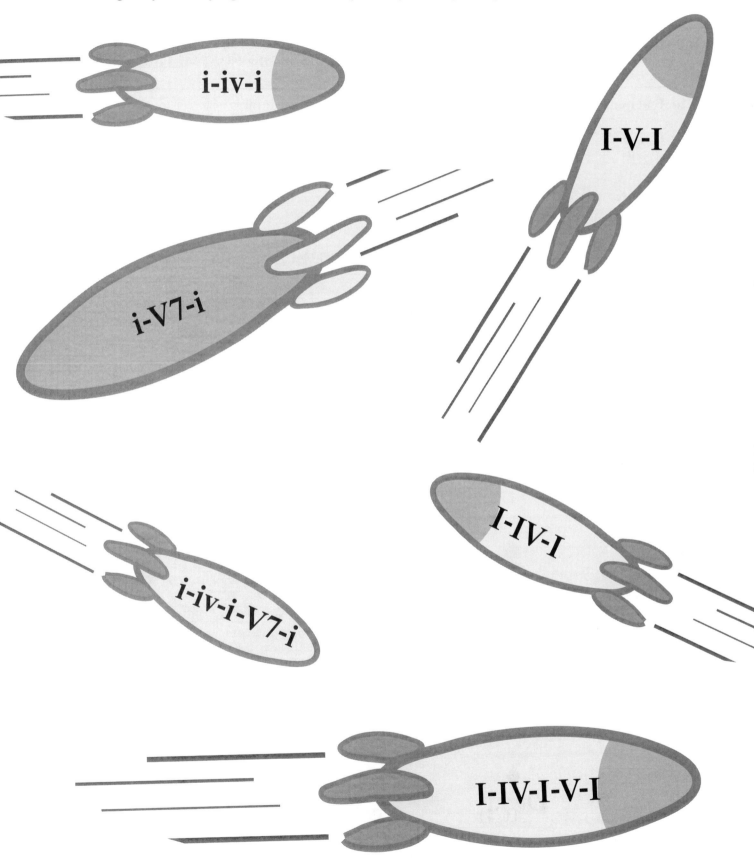

Review Game

TRAVEL IN THE TIME MACHINE!
A journey through the major and minor regions of musical space.

Directions: Beginning at the key of C, travel to each of the keys on the clock below.
As your teacher points to a key, play that arpeggio and the I-IV-I-V7-I cadence.

Note to Teacher: You may ask the student to play either major or minor.

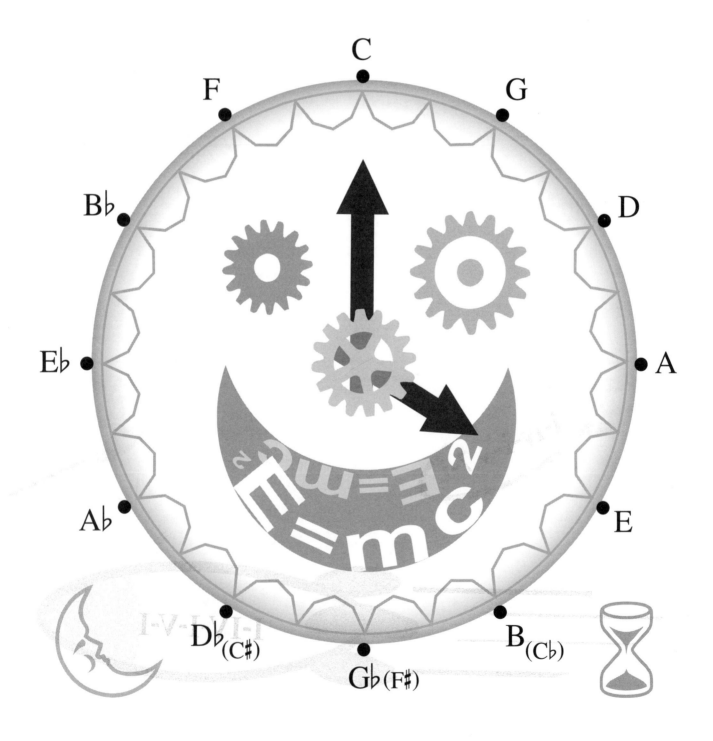